TABLE OF CONTENTS

DISCLAIMER AND TERMS OF USE AGREEMENT:

Introduction

Chapter 1 - Real Life Scenario

Chapter 2 - Forensic Tools

Chapter 3 - Who owns a phone number?

Address and phone of a person

How to find out the merchant ID of the company

Tracking down violators

Recording phone conversations

   900 numbers

   800 number ownership

   Phone number ownership

   Who is at this Address?

Chapter 4 - Find out who called you

   Locating a company

I Have a Special Gift for My Readers

Meet the Author

Cyber Daters BEWARE
Beware of Online Dating Site's Cyber Criminals
©Copyright 2013 by Dr. Noah Pranksky

DISCLAIMER AND TERMS OF USE AGREEMENT:

(Please Read This Before Using This Book)

This information is for educational and informational purposes only. The content is not intended to be a substitute for any professional advice, diagnosis, or treatment.

The author and publisher of this book and the accompanying materials have used their best efforts in preparing this book.

The author and publisher make no representation or warranties with respect to the accuracy, applicability, fitness, or completeness of the contents of this book. The information contained in this book is strictly for educational purposes. Therefore, if you wish to apply ideas contained in this book, you are taking full responsibility for your actions.

The author and publisher disclaim any warranties (express or implied), merchantability, or fitness for any particular purpose. The author and publisher shall in no event be held liable to any party for any direct, indirect, punitive, special, incidental or other consequential damages arising directly or indirectly from any use of this material, which is provided "as is", and without warranties. As always, the advice of a competent legal, tax, accounting, medical or other professional should be sought where applicable.

The author and publisher do not warrant the performance, effectiveness or applicability of any sites listed or linked to in this book. All links are for information purposes only and are not warranted for content, accuracy or any other implied or explicit purpose. No part of this may be copied, or changed in any format, or used in any way other than what is outlined within this course under any circumstances. Violators will be prosecuted.

This book is © Copyrighted by ePubWealth.com.

Introduction

There has never been another time in human history where women have become more aggressively pursued targets of various predators – from identity theft to sexual addicts and deviants, not to mention sociopaths like rapist and murderers.

With the advent of the Internet in 1989, women are now leaving themselves exposed to more of the predatory elements than ever before.

Allow me just a moment for a small commercial here.

ForensicsNation's main business is in commercial applications with corporate clients and involves everything from corporate espionage to hacking into industrial control systems (ICS) and much more such as network intrusions, piracy, fraud, terrorism, etc.

None of what we do on a commercial basis is available to the general public.

Our website is designed to provide resources and information for the general public allowing individuals to become "amateur sleuths".

All of the products, web resources, and information is readily available to individuals and is mostly FREE!

As Chief Forensics Investigator for ForensicsNation, I write articles, white papers, ebooks, etc for the 32-divisions that make up Applied Web Info/Neternatives.com.

The reason why I bring these facts up is because Neternatives provides FREE resources on a variety of protection and privacy topics and they are available to anyone who wants them.

I strongly advise you to take advantage of all of their FREE resources. I wrote a good many of them so you know they are excellent (lol).

Okay, lets' begin...

Chapter 1 - Real Life Scenario

I want to paint a real-life scenario for you. It is an actual case study taken from our company's file but the names have been changed. Unfortunately, it is only one of thousands happening around the world. Strap on your seat belts, this ain't gonna be pretty.

Sally is a business executive for a large insurance company in Las Vegas, Nevada. Her busy schedule causes her social life a lot to be desired so armed with the advice from some of her girlfriends she tries a popular online dating service. Her friends offer some sound advice to "protect" herself from the "jerks" and she writes them all down and follows each one to a tee.

She posts her profile and photo and soon her inbox is flooded with emails from guys that like her "stuff." Most of them she labels as "losers" and junks them but one catches her eye. His name is Bob and he is cute, has a good job and says all the right things.

She emails a response back to Bob using the online dating platform's response email and not her personal email and begins a month-long email conversation with Bob.

After a month Bob asks to meet her personally and just to be safe, suggests Starbucks in one of the local malls. Sally feels safe; after all it is a public place and Bob has none of her personal information.

Unbeknownst to Sally, Bob is a predator and he is very good at what he does.

They meet at Starbucks and Sally soon realizes that Bob is a very nice guy. He is funny, attentive and a true gentleman. He doesn't ask any personal information and keeps the conversation light. When she gets up to leave, he politely shakes her hand and asks if she would have dinner with him. She agrees to a time and place and they agree to meet each other at the restaurant.

Good so far?

Sally walks back to her car unaware that Bob has followed her and has written down her license plate.

When Bob gets home, he runs her plate through an online service (**Docusearch:** http://www.docusearch.com/) and now knows where Sally lives and her driver's license number.

Sally keeps her dinner date with Bob and again he is charming. As they get up to leave, Bob hands her his business card and tells her to call him if she feels comfortable doing it; otherwise, just email him.

Nice, eh? What a guy?

Sally thanks him and leaves and sees no harm with Bob having her cell number so she calls him when she gets home to tell him she got home safely and they talk for about 15-minutes.

Let's back up a minute...

Bob gave Sally his business card with his cell phone number on it. Unbeknownst to Sally, the number listed is not his cell phone number but a MagicJack number (anybody can buy a MagicJack and it doesn't take any personal information to set it up) that is forwarded to his real cell phone number. His cell phone was purchased from the Walmart StraightTalk program; which also doesn't take any personal information, no contract and is disposable. He changes the phone and the number often. He is also careful not to purchase a smartphone since they have GPS tracking locators built into them (law enforcement catches a lot of bad guys from the GPS locator chips in their cell phones) and always purchases the inexpensive analog phone for $39.95.

Now let's get back to the story...

Bob now has everything he needs to do his dirty deed. Bob has a lot of work ahead of him so let's follow him for a bit and see what Bob does.

The next day, Bob goes to the nearest Starbucks and uses their free Wi-Fi wireless service. He grabs a flash drive from his desk first and puts it in his pocket.

On his flash drive he has stored all of the "tools" of his trade. Even though he is operating on his laptop, through a public wireless service that cannot be traced back to him, on his flash drive he has a program that hides his computer's IP address (http://bit.ly/ow4WZD) and uses a proxy service just to be on the safe side (http://proxy-heaven.blogspot.com/).

Now Bob is completely invisible…at least Bob thinks so.

Armed with Sally's cell phone number he plants a spyware program on her cell phone that spies on her voice calls, her text messages, her photos and anything else stored on it (http://j.mp/pn7DK9). He does this simply by calling Sally's cell phone number and in 30-seconds marries the spyware to her phone. He doesn't even need to be in possession of here phone to put the spyware on it; it is all done over the phone.

Using the GPS locator chip in Sally's phone he is able to track her location and her movements (like this one in the UK….I purposely am not giving out the one for the USA for obvious reasons): http://www.world-tracker.com/v4/

Sally had long given up using the online dating site's email service and has been emailing Bob back and forth from her personal and business email accounts. From her personal emails, Bob now knows her computer's IP address and Internet ISP service. He hacks into her computer and plants a keylogger program (http://bit.ly/ufx533).

Now he can read all of her keystrokes as she logs into her online banking, credit card accounts and personal brokerage accounts. Soon he has all of her banking details, credit card numbers and brokerage assets.

From her business computer, he now knows her insurance company's LAN network and hacks into it (I will not give out the program Bob uses to conduct his hacking) armed with the login and password he gained from her personal computer keylogger program. Sally likes to work from home and dials into her office computer often. Once inside, he accesses her personal employment file from the HR department and Bob now knows Sally's social security number as well as all of her personal data.

Bob has been busy but his dirty deeds haven't even begun yet. Can you guess what Bob is going to do next? I think you can guess. To be brief, Sally lost all of her liquid assets from her bank account, brokerage account and credit cards. After Bob stole Sally's identity, he open up 12-credit card accounts, maxed out the credit lines and then closed up shop and moved on to a new location.

Sally became aware of what Bob had done about a week later but never knew it was Bob. She filed a police report but they told her that very rarely did they catch any of these hackers nor did they commit any resources to finding them. Sally was devastated and angry, mainly because she was clueless as to how it was done and also upset that the police would not do anything about it.

So what did Sally do? Sally was fortunate to have a friend that worked for ForensicsNation. Sally called her friend's contact and ForensicsNation open a case file. It took 3-months to track Bob down. We found him in Miami, Florida in the middle of another one of his scams. He was one surprised dude when he was picked up by law enforcement authorities.

At his trial (the Feds prosecuted him since he had gone across state lines and had hacked into a Federally-insured bank to gain access to Sally's accounts.), we testified behind a screen to protect our identities. Bob is now doing 25-years in a Federal Corrections Institute.

*****

What could Sally had one short of staying off her computer completely to protect herself? Let's go through it item by item.

First, NEVER give out your personal cell number unless you thoroughly know the individual. Receive calls only on your cell phone that you know people. Get a disposable cell phone with a changeable number:

Unlock or "Jail Break your cell phone: http://bit.ly/pizQvj

Prepaidonline: http://bit.ly/o8uSPs

CellHub: http://bit.ly/odI6Md

LetsTalk: http://bit.ly/rik2Qm

RingCentral: http://bit.ly/ntIPay

Google Voice: http://www.google.com/voice

PhoneSale: http://bit.ly/pHYVB9

GSM Nation: http://bit.ly/nfvJFF

StraightTalk: http://www.straighttalk.com

Forward your voicemail: http://bit.ly/pHYVB9

Protect all your cell phones with this product:

http://usa.kaspersky.com/products-services/home-computer-security/mobile-security

Be aware of your surroundings. Become a trained observer. Go here for the training:

http://store.payloadz.com/details/781948-ebooks-science-applied-mind-sciences.html

Protect your computer's information from hackers:

http://www.truecrypt.org/docs/

http://www.endoacustica.com/index_en.htm

http://www.openpgp.org/

Stay anonymous when you surf the web:

Anonymouse: http://anonymouse.org/

Hide MY IP: http://bit.ly/ow4WZD

Identity Cloaker: http://bit.ly/ofl1rs

Anonymizer: http://bit.ly/oJGbzF

HotspotShield: http://www.hotspotshield.com/

StartPage: http://www.startpage.com.

Tor Project: https://www.torproject.org/.

Pretty Good Privacy (PGP) http://www.pgpi.org/

Freenet Project: http://freenetproject.org/

Use an encrypted email service:

Hushmail: http://www.hushmail.com/

Protect your computer's firewall:

http://www.comodo.com/

Use phone services that are difficult to hack:

Skype: http://www.skype.com/;

Zfone: http://zfoneproject.com/.

Xmeeting: http://xmeeting.sourceforge.net/pages/xmeeting.php

MagicJack: http://www.magicjack.com/

Private Phone Carrier – DPI: http://www.dpiteleconnect.com/public/

Social Mobile Messaging - Jangl: http://www.jangl.com/

Be sure to check this site out: https://xerobank.com/

*****

Here are some valuable resources that you can use to become an amateur sleuth

Chapter 2 - Forensic Tools

File Viewers: http://www.jasc.com

Image Viewers: http://www.cerious.com

Password Crackers: http://www.atstake.com

Format-independent Text Search: dtsearch: http://www.dtsearch.com

Drive Imaging: Norton Utilities' Ghost: http://www.symantec.com

Forensics Toolkit: http://www.foundstone.com

ForensiX: http://www.all.net

EnCase Forensic: http://www.encase.com

Forensic Computer Systems: http://www.forensic-computers.com

NetScanTools Pro: http://www.netscantools.com

Chapter 3 - Who owns a phone number?

The fastest, easiest and simplest way to find out who owns any phone number is Phone Search Central: http://www.phonesearchcentral.com/

If you want to do things the harder way (which is NOT worth the time), FoneFinder; http://www.fonefinder.net will tell you which company owns the phone number. You can then subpoena that company to get the owner of the phone number.

Address and phone of a person

PeopleFinders: http://www.peoplefinders.com is a reasonable service. Their "people search subscription" works reasonably well, finding all sorts of things, including some things that are completely wrong. Don't use this for 800 number reverse searches...I never got anything even remotely useful from those (and they will reverse the charge on these automatically if you make a mistake). For cell phone numbers doing a reverse search, it will tell you only the name of the subscriber; and the location of the number when it was originally assigned; no address of the person. It is annoying that on every search it prompts you to sign up for a $16.95 "savings" program. The link to sign up is huge. The link to say "no thanks" is below it in small type, and somewhat hard to find. I did a criminal search on a guy I knew was convicted and it wouldn't tell me what county it was in, but it did find it. This service is a bit pricey, but may be your lowest cost option if you've exhausted the alternatives.

How to find out the merchant ID of the company

You may have to put a small $ transaction through in order to get complete info. Having a rejected transaction may only give you the "name" of the vendor as it would appear on your statement which can be quite obscure and often bogus.

Bank of America ShopSafe: https://www.bankofamerica.com/banking-information/faq/credit-cards/faq.go is the best option. You can generate a onetime number (including the 3 digit code) that is tied to your credit card and you can set a dollar and time limit on that unique card number. But once a merchant charges to that card, it is locked to that merchant. So it is really safe.

A Visa Buxx: http://usa.visa.com/personal/cards/prepaid/visa_buxx.html number or a **Visa reloadable card:**

http://usa.visa.com/personal/cards/prepaid/prepaidcard.jsp?it=l2|/personal/cards/prepaid/visa_buxx.html|Visa%20Reloadable is another choice. Keep the amount in the account really low. When they try to charge your card, you can find out their merchant ID but ONLY if the transaction goes through! If it doesn't go through, then you only get the info that would appear on your bill (which could be bogus and it is not traceable). There are monthly fees though even if you don't use these cards. The B of A ShopSafe has no additional fees.

Tracking down violators

http://www.tcpalaw.com/free/track.htm

This page at tcpalaw.com is an excellent resource of all sorts of information including forms to get PO Box information.

Recording phone conversations

I use Personal call Recorder from www.digital-loggers.com. I use the free WavePad from www.nch.com.au and sample at 16000 and save it in MP3 Constant bit rate CBR 16kbps (high quality). For lower quality and fast saves, capture at 8K and save in .wav format, PCM, 8kHz, 8 bit, mon, 7Kb/sec. Be sure it is legal first:

900 numbers
Number Administration System

http://www.nanpa.com/nas/public/form900MasterReport.do?method=display900MasterReport shows the responsible organization for each number. You then send a subpoena to the company to find out who owns it.

800 number ownership
As far as finding the resp org, in theory your long distance carrier should be willing to supply that for you. Ameritech has an automated service at 800-337-4194; they typically give a service number associated with the RespOrg, which you can then call to find out who the RespOrg actually is. A third method: "If you don't know who to subpoena, use the RespOrg services or go to: http://www.fonefinder.net (Note: this works for non-toll free numbers too!) and find out the provider and then go to:
http://www.nanpa.com/number_resource_info/carrier_id_codes.html

(Download the "Feature Group D CIC assignments" zipfile) to get their contact info. Call to ask who to send a subpoena to, and then send it.

If you have a login, you can go right to the source: http://www.sms800.com

For Canadian numbers: see CO Code Availability: http://www.cgnc.ca/mapcodes.htm

With respect to subpoenas to RespOrg, I've found that you can generally fax the subpoena to them and simply ask that they fax the answer back. In three of three cases, they have simply faxed the information back to me.

Phone number ownership
Abika services: Find out who owns a number or who is calling you:

http://www.abika.com/Reports/FindPhoneNumbers.htm

Abika offers a very comprehensive set of searches and is very similar to Docusearch. Unlike Docusearch they can trace the source of a fax call into your phone number. This is the only service we know of that lets you do that without your having to change your incoming fax line into an 800 number (they can't block their callerID if you have an incoming 800 number).

The way their service works is that you forward your fax line to their number and they forward the call back to your number instantly. In the process, they pick off the callerID that you can't get. So let's say you get 10 faxes a day. You just note the time you receive each fax and correlate it to the list they give you of phone numbers that called you at the same time. So you can identify the number of every single fax you got over any time period! It's called the "Trace Phone Calls" Search.

The Abika "Trace Phone Calls" service is highly recommended because you get the phone numbers of each of the junk faxers that called you regardless of how they are trying to block their number. Then you can use the other Abika searches to find out who they really are (billing name and address, etc). Then you can sue the sender of the faxes. This is particularly useful for pump and dump faxes and the 900 number "we want your opinion" faxes because these faxes generally never identify who is sending them (since they want to avoid lawsuits) and if they have an opt-out number, it is generally http://www.blocklist.com and that's totally useless since blocklist doesn't identify individual clients...they just give the list to all their clients. So you can't sue blocklist and blocklist can't tell you who sent the fax. In fact, someone can just list the blocklist numbers and not even be a blocklist client! So that's why the Abika service is so important and it's the only one we know of that does this.

The cost is $79.96 ($69.98 plus 9.98 processing charge) for the first month; $10 for 1 month extensions. You get 100 minutes of talk time free with your initial order. You can buy additional 60 minutes of talk time for $10 each. For Canada, Hawaii, Alaska and Puerto Rico you get 50 minutes of talk time free with your order. You can buy additional 30 minutes of talk time for $10 each.

Note: You will probably not be able to forward back to the original number. This will depend on the local phone or Cell Phone Company and often on the area, even within the same phone company. They have a database of the phone/cell companies and the areas where it works and it does not. For areas where it gives a busy signal the call has to be returned to a different phone number or voicemail.

But for fax lines, if you don't have a second line handy or a fax machine that timestamps when the fax was really received (I don't have either), the best option is to do what I did and just forward my fax number to Abika's call center and then have them forward it the phone number of an efax service you sign up for such as http://www.efax.com. So you don't have to have another phone line installed, and you get an electronic record of everything, including accurate receipt times that you can then correlate to their call logs. And you can set everything up instantly (the efax number is instant; call forwarding may take a couple of business days to add).

Abika can immediately tell you of the caller's origin number and billing address. You either call or email them for the info. This is part of the "Trace Phone Call" monthly service. So to do a live trace, you must do the same as described above, i.e., forward your number to them and have it forwarded back. As long as the call is 5 seconds or longer, you'll know who called you.

The service works virtually 100% of the time, even if the number is "out of area" or blocked and even when they were unidentifiable by callerID, *69, and *57. Basically, they get the ANI (Automatic Number Identification) information that certain businesses get. Getting ANI delivered real-time to your home or office requires installation of digital equipment and a separate digital line, and programming at the CO. So Abika is the quick and easy way to accomplish the same result (getting the ANI information), but without the hassle, cost, or time delay.

Here's what they write:

We have had hundreds of customers who have used our call trace. If you would like to test us out, I can activate trace for a number you specify and you can ask any of your associates to dial that number from any unlisted, anonymous phone number or even using *69 and check us out. We will trace the origin number for all calls that originate in US and Canada. The proof is in the pudding. The test will speak for itself. (Can we get the $20 for winning the bet?)

Regarding our price list, we do not have fixed pricing of our products. Our prices are dynamic and vary according to the complexity of the various searches we offer. Where is the price list? Each search is unique and gets the attention it requires. Prices vary depending on whose and what information you are searching as some information is easier (cheaper) to search and some more difficult (expensive). Once you fill out the search form with the search criteria and click "next" you will see the prices for that particular search. If the information is easy to search then that particular search is listed as FREE! You can try any of our searches. **All of them have a money back guarantee for inaccurate information found.** As a businessperson you would be interested in knowing that the Wall Street Journal got the full report on Richard Scrushy (ex CEO) of Healthsouth's suspect activities from us even before anyone else in the media or investment community suspected anything. The time when WSJ got the full report Healthsouth was a high flying stock. In most of the searches we offer, we have the best sources for the information. We have even had a senior editor of People Magazine, a few magazine reporters and news anchors of a couple of local TV stations use us to get information for some of their stories and personal needs.

Here are some testimonials from customers who agreed to publish their feedback: http://www.abika.com/help/feedback.htm

You may be interested to know that we offer a similar service to trace emails and instant messages. Emails and IM traces are available for the whole of N. America, W. Europe, India, South Africa and the Pacific Rim Countries including Australia and Japan. I wonder when many of the so called tech gurus say that emails and IM's are untraceable. We have conducted thousands of these traces with a success rate of more than 98%. A few major corporations use us to trace emails and IM's.

If you have any more questions or need any more information please do not hesitate to contact us online. help@abika.com. Or if you choose you can call us at: 720-207-0362.

Docusearch: http://www.docusearch.com/

Use Docusearch to lookup License plate owners, social security numbers lookup (for creditors) and find out who owns an 800 number, regular phone number, and more. Expensive (well under $100), but some stuff you can only get this way. If they can't find it, there's no charge. Also use Ameritech's automated RespOrg ID service: 800-337-4194.

Call trap procedure

This is guaranteed to get your offender. Have the phone company put a "trap" on the line, make note of when the calls came in. You must have the EXACT time of each call. Then I report it by calling the Annoyance and Tracking line. For SBC, the number is 800-698-7223. After you get two faxes from the same sender, if they can't get a number, then they can put traps at the remote location and eventually you get them. Hit 0 to speak a live person when calling the SBC number.

Here is some more info on call trap: Caller ID and My Privacy:

https://www.privacyrights.org/fs/fs19-cid.htm

The number for the SBC Annoyance call bureau is 925-867-8101, for example. Here's some slightly conflicting advice: Now *all* calls are logged by the LEC's (Local Exchange Carrier) computers. Ask them (via subpoena) for a call detail report (CDR) for all calls into and out from your number on the affected date. *ALL* the phone companies have this data... most for 90 days of history or more. If they tell you they don't, they are lying

Accurint.com: http://www.accurint.com/

25-cents a search. Highly useful for tracking down people, even with unlisted phone numbers. Accurint uses a name, past address, phone number or Social Security Number to obtain the current name, address and phone number of targeted subjects. Be careful that you don't lookup someone you don't have a legal reason to lookup, or you can be sued by that person. So if you are looking up information for a lawsuit, that's ok.

Whois Source - Wildcard Domain Search Lookup

http://www.whois.sc/. I have a silver membership here. It's totally worth it if you look up website registration. There are other lots of other reverse lookup tools here if you are a member.

Advanced Research, Inc. - Background Investigations, Asset Searches, Telephone Records, Locates: http://www.advsearch.com/

They will find a bank account owned by the debtor, bank balances for all accounts in a given bank, bank transactions, credit card transactions, Canadian phone records, etc. Even international bank account searches. You can find out where the person is currently employed. Searches that is not available on the traditional databases.

MelissaData address lookups: http://www.melissadata.com/Lookups/index.htm

Lookup address related thing

Ancillary Service Endorsements:

http://w5.melissadata.com/cgi-bin/search.asp?pnf=appnotes/ancserv.htm

"Return service requested" (preferred) or "Address service requested" is both ways to find a new address or confirm an existing address. See this page for a description of each type of endorsement.

Free People Search - Find People - Free People Locator - Find People Free, Skip Tracing, Trace People at skipease.com variety of people search: http://www.skipease.com/.

Find anyone! We'll locate missing persons, debtors, assets, and employment (skiptracepros.com): http://www.skiptracepros.com/ Pay service but worth it.

Satellite photos - You can search by latitude/longitude, street address, zip code, or well known locations:

http://mapper.acme.com/

http://terraserver.microsoft.com/

International business name search

General Guides:

Company Registrars - Register of Companies - Trade, Industry

http://www.scottishlaw.org.uk/corporate/registrars.html

International Company name search

http://www.damonlegal.com/link_to_forms.htm

International phone number search

International phonebooks directory

http://www.phonebooks.com/international-phone-book.html

International Telephone Numbers Directory - City, State, Country Phone Number Look-up

http://www.searchdetective.net/International_phone_number.html

Batch reverse phone number

Use Accurint batch mode or a service from infoUSA.com.

http://list.infousa.com/cgi-bin/abicgi/abicgi.pl?bas_session={bas_session}&bas_elements=4&bas_vendor=190000&bas_type=LC&bas_page=6999&bas_action=dataproc

ABA number lookup

ABA routing number verification. Free bank routing number search tool:

http://yourfavorite.com/checkwriter/verify.htm

Bank account balance: See if funds are in the account you want to levy!

http://bettercheck.com/

TCPALaw investigation tools

A great list: Tracking down violators

http://www.tcpalaw.com/free/track.htm

Report bogus domain information

Bogus information in the domain registration in violation of ICANN regulations. Registrars are required to ensure that registration data is complete & accurate. You will have to subpoena the registrar for the information on who paid for the registration. You should also download and capture all information off of the web site and look to see who hosts the web page, as they can also be subpoenaed for customer data. In the meantime, you can report incomplete or inaccurate domain registration information here: http://wdprs.internic.net/

CorpAmerica Corporate filings

http://www.corpamerica.com/cam/Error.html?pageNotFound=%2Fcam%2Fproducts_%26_services%2F

If you want to find out who the officers are, etc. you can order a "plain" copy of corporate records for any state in the US and some foreign corporations. See also: Division of Corporations - Authorized Direct Web Vendors:

http://www.corp.delaware.gov/directwebvend.shtml

Yellow pages, white pages, and reverse number lookup:

http://www.anywho.com/

http://www.argali.com/

Forward and reverse phone number lookup. This is a downloadable FREE tool that searches public databases.

FCC unsolicited fax orders and search:
http://transition.fcc.gov/eb/tcd/ufax.html

Enter the name your favorite spammer and read what the FCC has done about them. Our favorite spammer, fax.com has 6 separate FCC citations on this page alone! This site uses the search engine that I invented when I was CEO of Infoseek, by the way. The FCC citations explain the law much better than anything I've seen on other sites. Read a few of them to educate yourself on the law.

GEEKTOOLS Whois Proxy

http://www.geektools.com/whois.php

Fast whois lookup

Cell Phone Magic:

http://www.cell-phone-numbers.com/

They will find out who owns a cell phone.

This online store offers a variety of searches and stuff you won't find anywhere else....like how to get keys for the car you want to levy. http://www.ioffer.com/

US SEARCH: http://www.ussearch.com/consumer/index.jsp

Similar to Docusearch

Offering nationwide and international investigative services, spy gadgets, safety and surveillance products, records research, criminal background checks and personal information verification services. Information retrieval for insurance companies, law firms, repossession agents, financial institutions, collection agencies, private investigators, bounty hunters, process servers, bail bondsmen, businesses, spouses and parents.

UPS Store Locator/ mail drop mailbox mail box location

Actually what you ALWAYS do when you have any address of any perpetrator is simply first go to the UPS Store Locations search page

http://go.vicinity.com/upsnew/prxStart.dsp

http://go.vicinity.com/mbe/prxStart.dsp

http://www.semaphorecorp.com/cgi/form.html

Excellent maildrop search: Mail boxes - remailing services. Directory of mail drops and mail boxes: http://www.maildropguide.com/go/

Who is at this Address?
If I have an address and I am not sure what it is, or if it's even a real address, then I always go to http://www.usps.com and look up the address and the post office that delivers to the address. Then I call that post office and ask them if they know what's located at that address. I ask if it is a residential address, or if it's an

office building of some sort. I ask them if they know if the address is a Commercial Mail Receiving Agency (CMRA) like a Mailboxes Etc or UPS Store. The post office is not required to answer these types of questions, but they can if they want to. I'd say 90% of the time they tell me what I need to know.

FEIN number lookup

Federal Employer ID Number can found here if it is registered: http://wwwKnowx.com

FEIN Number information Search Corporation Tax ID Number

https://www.knowx.com/fein/search.jsp

Otherwise http://www.dnb.com may work.

AutoTrackXP: https://clear.thomsonreuters.com/

Very comprehensive searches! Requires a subscription agreement and qualification.

Reverse Phone Directory - Find Name and Street Address from Telephone Number

http://www.reversephonedirectory.com/

Reverse phone number lookup:

http://www.infospace.com/ispace/ws/index

Find out who owns a phone number

Reverse Address Directory - Lookup Street Address Find Person's Name and Telephone Number to Locate People and See Who Lives There.

http://www.reverseaddress.com/

Craig Ball's Sampler of Informal Discovery Links:

http://www.craigball.com/hotlinks.html

A pretty extensive list of resources

ScreenNow: https://screennow.lexisnexis.com/pub/

Get all sorts of info on a person.

Net Detective 2001 people search utility software- HDP Corporate Website

http://ndet.jeanharris.com/

Essentially a bunch of semi-useful hyperlinks, all categorized for you

OnlineDetective.com - unlisted phone numbers dmv records detectives personal public records investigate anything and more!

http://www.onlinedetective.com/

Seems to be similar to net detective

SuperPages.com: http://www.superpages.com/

A search at superpages.com (hint: I usually look for the category "mail" at the particular address, then if that doesn't turn up a mail drop, search for any businesses at the address) turns up, for example, 5401 Chimney Rock Apartments 5401 Chimney Rock Road, Houston, TX 77081 (713) 661-3790

Canada phone number lookup

http://www.canada411.ca/

Canada's 411

United States Postal Service - ZIP + 4 Lookup

https://www.usps.com/

Handy when they don't give you enough info to confirm you got the right company.

GNU wget: http://www.gnu.org/software/wget/wget.html

I used this to grab a complete copy of the fax.com website so that they couldn't change it.

Find out who owns a PO Box: http://www.junkfax.org/fax/misc/pobox.htm

Some popular techniques to find out the owner of PO Box

Telephone Prefix location: http://www.thedirectory.org/pref/

If you have a phone number like (650) 423-xxxx, it will tell you where that phone is.

CCS International Ltd: Surveillance, Counter surveillance and Hi-Tech Spy and Security Products: http://www.spyzone.com/

GSM, CELLULAR, COMPUTER, FAX MONITORING

http://www.gcomtech.com/

Due to federal law, you must be in law enforcement to get access to this site.

ZoomInfo: http://www.zoominfo.com/

This is a free site where you can find lots of information about a person or a company gathered from analyzing web pages. Very impressive!

Chapter 4 - Find out who called you

Use the call trace feature offered by the phone company. I did a *57 and got a "successful" trace, FWIW, plus an announcement that for $8 (plus tax and tip, no doubt) I can even have it reported to the police. For $8, they can record the number. Then if you take action, you subpoena the phone company for the call info, and if it is a subscriber of that phone company, you get info on the caller as well. If it's not a subscriber of the phone co, you generally get who the local carrier is so you know who to subpoena for the subscriber info. If you were to have the number but want the subscriber info, and issued a subpoena to SWB, they would charge you a $25 fee for the record search. When you do a call trace, you get the whole shebang for $8. I've done call traces when I have the subscriber's name and number, but want a) a sworn affidavit from the phone company saying that the call was made from number "X" to my number "Y" at a specific date and time, and b) if it is from a SWB customer, full ID of the calling party, including name & address where the service is installed. All for $8, much cheaper than issuing a subpoena for records after the fact, and with more info.

Locating a company
http://www.residentagentinfo.com page links to all the state corp. search pages on the net. Pretty helpful, if you still can't find it

http://www.checkemout.com/corporation_go.html has a nationwide corp/dba search for $39.00.

http://www.freelancesecurity.com will let you have private PI's bid for a service you describe.

Can We Tape: http://www.rcfp.org/taping/

Rules regarding taping of phone conversations in each state.

*****

If you remember anything please remember this: YOU ARE NEVER INVISIBLE ON THE NET! You may think you are but there are companies like ForensicsNation that have software programs that can find you anywhere. I sincerely hope this has helped you better protect yourself. If you have any questions write to me at lee.benton@neternatives.com.

I Have a Special Gift for My Readers

I appreciate my readers for without them I am just another author attempting to make a difference. If my book has made a favorable impression please leave me an honest review. Thank you in advance for you participation.

My readers and I have in common a passion for the written word as well as the desire to learn and grow from books.

My special offer to you is a massive ebook library that I have compiled over the years. It contains hundreds of fiction and non-fiction ebooks in Adobe Acrobat PDF format as well as the Greek classics and old literary classics too.

In fact, this library is so massive to completely download the entire library will require over 5 GBs open on your desktop.

Use the link below and scan all of the ebooks in the library. You can select the ebooks you want individually or download the entire library.

The link below does not expire after a given time period so you are free to return for more books rather than clog your desktop. And feel free to give the link to your friends who enjoy reading too.

I thank you for reading my book and hope if you are pleased that you will leave me an honest review so that I can improve my work and or write books that appeal to your interests.

Okay, here is the link…

http://tinyurl.com/special-readers-promo

PS: If you wish to reach me personally for any reason you may simply write to mailto:support@epubwealth.com.

I answer all of my emails so rest assured I will respond.

Meet the Author

Dr. Noah Pranksky is a research behavioral scientist for Applied Mind Sciences. His research involves many aspects of the human mind including relationships, energy psychology, and various protocols and modalities relating to treatment and cure of various mental maladies.

He and his wife Marianne reside in Portland, Oregon.

Visit some of his websites
http://www.AddMeInNow.com
http://www.AppliedMindSciences.com
http://www.BookbuilderPLUS.com
http://www.BookJumping.com
http://www.EmailNations.com
http://www.EmbarrassingProblemsFix.com
http://www.ePubWealth.com
http://www.ForensicsNation.com
http://www.ForensicsNationStore.com
http://www.FreebiesNation.com
http://www.HealthFitnessWellnessNation.com
http://www.Neternatives.com
http://www.PrivacyNations.com
http://www.RetireWithoutMoney.org
http://www.SurvivalNations.com
http://www.TheBentonKitchen.com
http://www.Theolegions.org
http://www.VideoBookbuilder.com

www.ingramcontent.com/pod-product-compliance
Lightning Source LLC
Chambersburg PA
CBHW051825170526
45167CB00005B/2165